Hot Math Topics

Problem Solving, Communication, and Reasoning

Estimation and Computation with Large Numbers

grade
5

Carole Greenes
Linda Schulman Dacey
Rika Spungin

Dale Seymour Publications®
Parsippany, New Jersey

Acknowledgment: The authors wish to acknowledge the outstanding contributions of Mali Apple in the production of the *Hot Math Topics* series. She has given careful attention to the content, design, and art, and helped shepherd the program through from its inception to its completion. Thank you, Mali.

Dale Seymour Publications
an imprint of Pearson Learning
299 Jefferson Road
Parsippany, New Jersey 07054-0480
www.pearsonlearning.com
800-321-3106

Editorial Manager: Carolyn Coyle
Project Editor: Mali Apple
Production/Manufacturing Director: Janet Yearian
Production/Manufacturing Manager: Karen Edmonds
Senior Production/Manufacturing Coordinator: Roxanne Knoll
Art Director: Jim O'Shea
Cover Design: Tracey Munz
Cover and Interior Illustrations: Jared Lee
Computer Graphics: Alan Noyes

ISBN 0-7690-0838-0

1 2 3 4 5 6 7 8 9 10-ML-04 03 02 01 00

This Book Is Printed
On Recycled Paper

Contents

Introduction

Why Was *Hot Math Topics* Developed?

The *Hot Math Topics* series was developed for several reasons:

- to offer students practice and maintenance of previously learned skills and concepts
- to enhance problem solving and mathematical reasoning abilities
- to build literacy skills
- to nurture collaborative learning behaviors

Practicing and maintaining concepts and skills

Although textbooks and core curriculum materials do treat the topics explored in this series, their treatment is often limited by the lesson format and the page size. As a consequence, there are often not enough opportunities for students to practice newly acquired concepts and skills related to the topics, or to connect the topics to other content areas. *Hot Math Topics* provides the necessary practice and mathematical connections.

Similarly, core instructional programs often do not do a very good job of helping students maintain their skills. Although textbooks do include reviews of previously learned material, they are frequently limited to sidebars or boxed-off areas on one or two pages in each chapter, with four or five exercises in each box. Each set of problems is intended only as a sampling of previously taught topics, rather than as a complete review. In the selection and placement of the review exercises, little or no attention is given to levels of complexity of the problems. By contrast, *Hot Math Topics* targets specific topics and gives students more experience with concepts and skills related to them. The problems are sequenced by difficulty, allowing students to hone their skills. And, because they are not tied to specific lessons, the problems can be used at any time.

Enhancing problem solving and mathematical reasoning abilities

Hot Math Topics presents students with situations in which they may use a variety of problem solving strategies, including

- designing and conducting experiments to generate or collect data
- guessing, checking, and revising guesses
- organizing data in lists or tables in order to identify patterns and relationships
- choosing appropriate computational algorithms and deciding on a sequence of computations
- using inverse operations in "work backward" solution paths

For their solutions, students are also required to bring to bear various methods of reasoning, including

- deductive reasoning
- inductive reasoning
- proportional reasoning

For example, to solve clue-type problems, students must reason deductively and make inferences about mathematical relationships in order to generate candidates for the solutions and to hone in on those that meet all of the problem's conditions.

To identify and continue a pattern and then write a rule for finding the next term in that pattern, students must reason inductively.

To compute unit prices and convert measurement units, students must reason proportionally.

To estimate or compare magnitudes of numbers, or to determine the type of number appropriate for a given situation, students must apply their number sense skills.

Building communication and literacy skills

Hot Math Topics offers students opportunities to write and talk about mathematical ideas. For many problems, students must describe their solution paths, justify their solutions, give their opinions, or write or tell stories.

Some problems have multiple solution methods. With these problems, students may have to compare their methods with those of their peers and talk about how their approaches are alike and different.

Other problems have multiple solutions, requiring students to confer to be sure they have found all possible answers.

Nurturing collaborative learning behaviors

Several of the problems can be solved by students working together. Some are designed specifically as partner problems. By working collaboratively, students can develop expertise in posing questions that call for clarification or verification, brainstorming solution strategies, and following another person's line of reasoning.

What Is in *Estimation and Computation with Large Numbers?*

This book contains 100 problems and tasks that focus on estimation and computation with large numbers. The mathematics content, the mathematical connections, the problem solving strategies, and the communication skills that are emphasized are described below.

Mathematics content

These problems and tasks require students to

- estimate sums, differences, products, and quotients
- estimate to solve problems when an exact answer is not required
- estimate distance, weight, and amount of time
- compute with large numbers
- identify values of digits in large numbers
- round numbers and amounts of money
- apply rate relationships to the solution of problems
- compute and interpret arithmetic averages
- identify the factors of numbers
- identify relationships among powers of 10
- compute perimeters, areas, and volumes of shapes

Mathematical connections

In these problems and tasks, connections are made to these other topic areas:

- algebra
- geometry
- measurement
- number theory
- statistics

Problem solving strategies

Estimation and Computation with Large Numbers problems and tasks offer students opportunities to use one or more of several problem solving strategies.

- **Formulate Questions:** When data are presented in displays or text form, students must pose one or more questions that can be answered using the given data.

- **Complete Problems:** When confronted with an incomplete problem, students must supply the missing information and then check that the solution makes sense.

- **Organize Information:** To ensure that all possible solution candidates for a problem are considered, students may have to organize information by making a list.

- **Guess, Check, and Revise:** In some problems, students have to identify candidates for the solution and then check whether those candidates match the conditions of the problem. If the conditions are not satisfied, other possible solutions must be generated and verified.

- **Identify and Continue Patterns:** To identify the next term or terms in a sequence, students have to recognize the relationship between successive terms and then generalize that relationship.

- **Use Logic:** Students have to reason deductively, from clues, to make inferences about the solution to a problem. They must reason proportionally to determine which of two buys is better and to convert measurement units. They have to reason inductively to continue numeric patterns.

Communication skills

Problems and tasks in *Estimation and Computation with Large Numbers* are designed to stimulate communication. As part of the solution process, students may have to

- describe their thinking steps
- describe patterns and rules
- find alternate solution methods and solution paths
- identify other possible answers
- formulate problems for classmates to solve
- compare estimates, solutions, and methods with classmates

These communication skills are enhanced when students interact with one another and with the teacher. By communicating both orally and in writing, students develop their understanding and use of the language of mathematics.

How Can *Hot Math Topics* Be Used?

The problems may be used as practice of newly learned concepts and skills, as maintenance of previously learned ideas, and as enrichment experiences for early finishers or more advanced students.

They may be used in class or assigned for homework. If used during class, they may be selected to complement lessons dealing with a specific topic or assigned every week as a means of keeping skills alive and well. Because the problems often require the application of various problem solving strategies and reasoning methods, they may also form the basis of whole-class lessons whose goals are to develop expertise with specific problem solving strategies or methods.

The problems, which are sequenced from least to most difficult, may be used by students working in pairs or on their own. The selection of problems may be made by the teacher or the students based on their needs or interests. If the plan is for students to choose problems, you may wish to copy individual problems onto card stock and laminate them, and establish a problem card file.

To facilitate record keeping, a Management Chart is provided on page 6. The chart can be duplicated so that there is one for each student. As a problem is completed, the space corresponding to that problem's number may be shaded. An Award Certificate is included on page 6 as well.

How Can Student Performance Be Assessed?

Estimation and Computation with Large Numbers problems and tasks provide you with opportunities to assess students'

- estimation ability
- computation abilities
- problem solving abilities
- communication skills

Observations

Keeping anecdotal records helps you to remember important information you gain as you observe students at work. To make observations more manageable, limit each observation to a group of from four to six students or to one of the areas noted above. You may find that using index cards facilitates the recording process.

Discussions

Many of the *Estimation and Computation with Large Numbers* problems and tasks allow for multiple answers or may be solved in a variety of ways. This built-in richness motivates students to discuss their work with one another. Small groups or class discussions are appropriate. As students share their approaches to the problems, you will gain additional insights into their content knowledge, mathematical reasoning, and communication abilities.

Scoring responses

You may wish to holistically score students' responses to the problems and tasks. The simple scoring rubric below uses three levels: high, medium, and low.

Portfolios

Having students store their responses to the problems in *Hot Math Topics* portfolios allows them to see improvement in their work over time. You may want to have them choose examples of their best responses for inclusion in their permanent portfolios, accompanied by explanations as to why each was chosen.

High	Medium	Low
• Solution demonstrates that the student knows the concepts and skills.	• Solution demonstrates that the student has some knowledge of the concepts and skills.	• Solution shows that the student has little or no grasp of the concepts and skills.
• Solution is complete and thorough.	• Solution is complete.	• Solution is incomplete or contains major errors.
• Student communicates effectively.	• Student communicates somewhat clearly.	• Student does not communicate effectively.

Students and the assessment process

Involving students in the assessment process is central to the development of their abilities to reflect on their own work, to understand the assessment standards to which they are held accountable, and to take ownership for their own learning. Young children may find the reflective process difficult, but with your coaching, they can develop such skills.

Discussion may be needed to help students better understand your standards for performance. Ask students such questions as, "What does it mean to communicate *clearly*?" "What is a *complete* response?" Some students may want to use the high-medium-low rubric to score their responses.

Participation in peer-assessment tasks will also help students to better understand the performance standards. In pairs or small groups, students can review each other's responses and offer feedback. Opportunities to revise work may then be given.

What Additional Materials Are Needed?

Calculators are required for solving several of the problems in *Estimation and Computation with Large Numbers* and may be useful in the solution of other problems as well.

Management Chart

Name _____

When a problem or task is completed, shade the box with that number.

1	2	3	4	5	6	7	8	9	10
11	12	13	14	15	16	17	18	19	20
21	22	23	24	25	26	27	28	29	30
31	32	33	34	35	36	37	38	39	40
41	42	43	44	45	46	47	48	49	50
51	52	53	54	55	56	57	58	59	60
61	62	63	64	65	66	67	68	69	70
71	72	73	74	75	76	77	78	79	80
81	82	83	84	85	86	87	88	89	90
91	92	93	94	95	96	97	98	99	100

Award Certificate

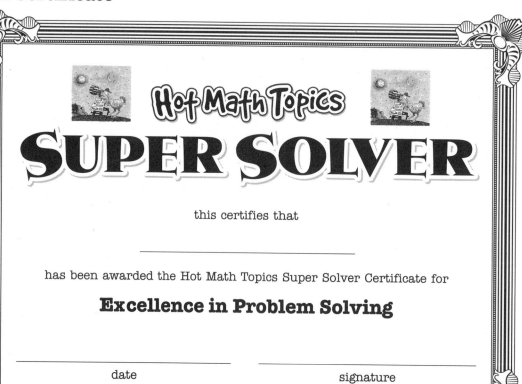

Hot Math Topics

SUPER SOLVER

this certifies that

_____

has been awarded the Hot Math Topics Super Solver Certificate for

Excellence in Problem Solving

_____   _____
date   signature

Problems
and Tasks

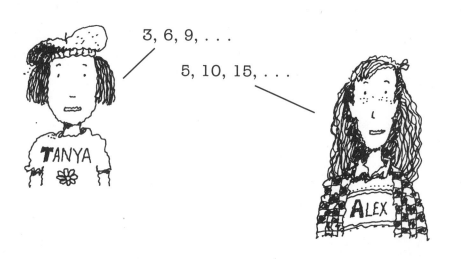

1

Tanya counted by 3s beginning with 3.

Alex counted by 5s beginning with 5.

If they continue counting to 1000, what numbers between 900 and 1000 will they both say?

Darryl was eating a jelly sandwich while doing his homework.

What's under the spilled jelly?

2

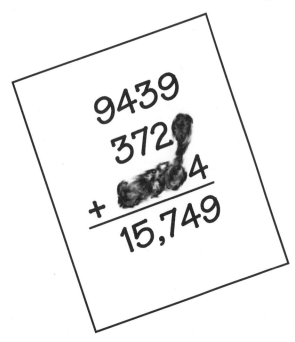

$$\begin{array}{r} 9439 \\ 372\_ \\ +\;\_4 \\ \hline 15{,}749 \end{array}$$

3

Lucy has $300.

Estimate: Can she buy a bicycle, helmet, water bottle, basket, and 2 pairs of bicycle shorts?

How do you know?

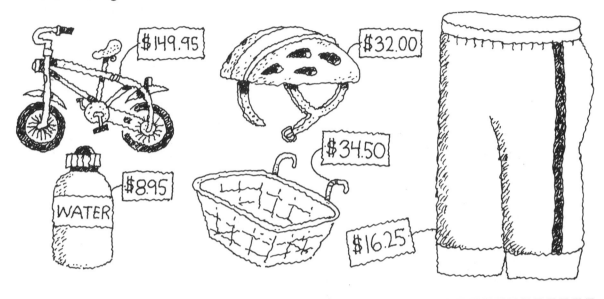

$149.95 $32.00

$8.95   WATER $34.50

$16.25

4

Write a multiplication or division clue for each "across" and "down" number.

Then do your puzzle to make sure it works.

Clues

Across	Down
1. 883×12	**1.**
3.	**2.**
4.	**5.**

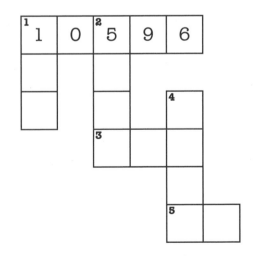

Ozzie wants to buy 29 tickets for the Shakespeare play.

Each ticket costs $32.

29 is about 30.
32 is about 30.
30 × 30 = 900.
I'll need $900 to
buy the tickets.

What do you think of Ozzie's reasoning?

- -

What's the number?

- The tenths digit is less than the hundredths digit.

- The ones digit is less than the tenths digit.

- The thousandths digit is 4 less than the hundredths digit.

9875.073   **1.483**

2614.312

603.417

600.695

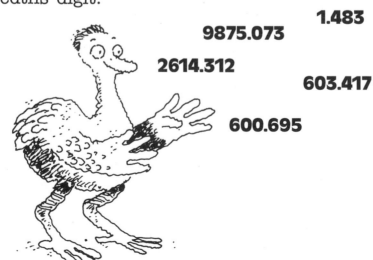

Use these numbers: 1000, 2000, 3000, 4000, 5000, and 6000.

Place each number in one of the ovals.

The sum of the 3 numbers on each side of the triangle must be 12,000.

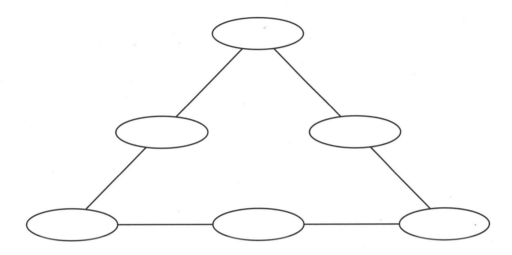

Work with a partner.

Name a 2-digit number.

Take turns multiplying by 2 or adding 10.

The first player to get closest to 1000, without going over 1000, is the winner.

Remember . . . don't go over 1000!

Use the facts to write a question for each answer on the sign.

9

Facts

- Max has 345 pennies and 854 nickels.
- Maddy has 2014 pennies and 325 dimes.

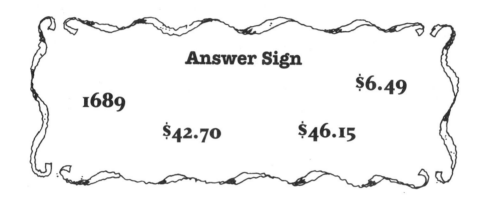

Answer Sign

1689

$6.49

$42.70 $46.15

- -

10

Six times some number is 3042.

What is 7 times this number?

Ms. Shah had $868.80.

- She used half of her money to buy a new television.
- She used half of what was left to pay her car loan.
- She used the remaining money to pay her electric bill.

How much was her electric bill?

The Gordon's car gets about 24 miles to a gallon of gasoline.

About how many gallons of gas will they need to drive round-trip from Boston to New York City?

Complete the grid.

The numbers in the ovals are the row and column sums.

2724.9		46.35	( )
	8687		(8706.05)
0.1		1094	(1143.6)
(2743.7)	(8740)	( )	

Rosa calculated the product 50 × 448 in her head.

Since 50 is half of 100, I will multiply by 100 and take half of my answer: 100 × 448 = 44,800, so 50 × 448 = 22,400.

Use Rosa's method to find 50 × 682.

15

One out of 7 people in North America is left-handed.

Mobile, Alabama, has a population of about 200,000.

To the nearest thousand, about how many people in Mobile are left-handed?

16

Here are 5 consecutive odd numbers:
21 23 25 27 29

Consecutive odd numbers are odd numbers that are in order.

The sum of 5 consecutive odd numbers is 305.

What is the first of the 5 odd numbers?

Check your answer.

Tell how you decided.

Play Wipe Out with a partner.

The object of the game is to replace ("wipe out") one digit of a 5-digit number with 0.

Rules

- Only one subtraction is allowed.

- Only the chosen digit is to change.

- Players take turns entering a 5-digit number and then asking the partner to "wipe out" one of the digits.

- Players receive 1 point for each digit "wiped out."

Example

Enter 15762 into a calculator.

Give the calculator to your partner.

Ask your partner to "wipe out" the 7.

I opened a book and added the page numbers on the facing pages.

The sum was 1237.

What were the page numbers?

Measure the length of your walking step.

About how many steps would you take to walk 1 mile?

Use your calculator to do the computation.

Compare your number with others in your class.

What is the average number of steps?

12 golf balls
$15.25

3 tennisballs
$4.60

2 baseballs
$3.75

Estimate the cost of

- 1 golf ball
- 1 tennis ball
- 1 baseball

21

2579 rounded to the nearest hundred is 2600.

2623 rounded to the nearest hundred is 2600.

How many whole numbers, rounded to the nearest hundred, equal 2600?

Tell how you decided.

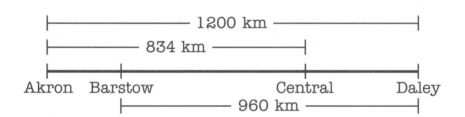

22

| ← 1200 km → |
| ← 834 km → |
Akron   Barstow   Central   Daley
| ← 960 km → |

What is the round-trip distance from Barstow to Central?

Put numbers in the shapes.

The same shapes have the same numbers.

Describe your thinking steps.

23

$$\begin{array}{r} \square\ \triangle\ 9 \\ \times\quad \triangle\ 4 \\ \hline 2\ 5\ 1\ 6 \\ 1\ 2\ 5\ 8 \\ \hline 1\ \hexagon\ 0\ 9\ 6 \end{array}$$

- -

24

You want to arrive at the airport 1 hour before your 8:15 A.M. flight.

You live 110 miles from the airport and expect to average 45 miles per hour on the drive there.

Estimate: At what time should you leave home?

Tell how you decided.

Work with a partner.

1. Write a number between 50,000 and 60,000.

2. Change the order of the digits to make a new number.

3. Use a calculator to find the difference between the 2 numbers.

4. Add the digits of the difference. If the sum has more than one digit, add the remaining digits until you get one digit.

What is the digit?

Do this 5 more times with different numbers.

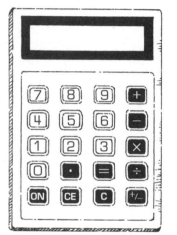

- -

Tell 2 ways to find the sum of the 16 numbers listed below.

Use one of your ways to find the sum.

101	102	103	104
1101	1102	1103	1104
2101	2102	2103	2104
3101	3102	3103	3104
4101	4102	4103	4104

The is equal to 3500.

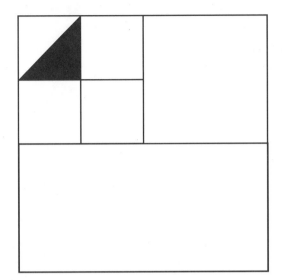

What is the value of the smallest square?

What is the value of the largest square?

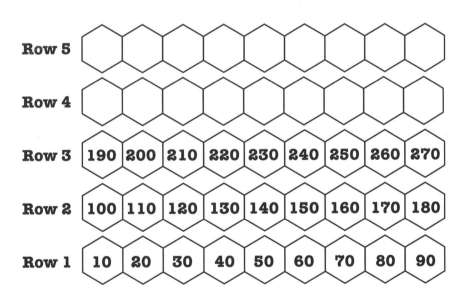

Row 5									
Row 4									
Row 3	190	200	210	220	230	240	250	260	270
Row 2	100	110	120	130	140	150	160	170	180
Row 1	10	20	30	40	50	60	70	80	90

The pattern continues.

In which row is 4580?

Tell how you know.

A brontosaurus dinosaur was about 85 feet long.

Imagine lots of students, your size, standing side by side.

How many students would be the same length as a brontosaurus?

© Dale Seymour Publications®

- -

About how many miles is it from Miami to Seattle?

Tell how you found your answer.

© Dale Seymour Publications®

Seattle

Denver

Mileage by Air
663 miles

Dallas

Miami

Write 2 more clues to identify one of the numbers on the sign.

Clues

- It is greater than 5245 + 5326.

- It is less than 10,545 + 7924.

- It is not equal to 20,000 − 4791.

- _____

- _____

Give your set of clues to a classmate.

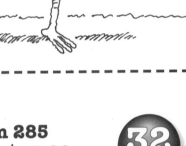

CompuMart will sell your school system 285 copies of *Treasure Math* for $6270 plus $15.98 for delivery.

Software Town will sell 285 copies for $21.50 each, with free delivery.

Which offer is the better buy?

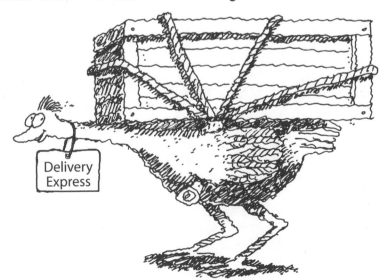

33

If that's true, what is  ?

34

Today is March 1.

It is 11 A.M.

The big baseball game is 1000 hours from today.

On what day is the game?

Race with a partner! Follow these rules:

- Write the start time. Each player makes up a multiplication example to fit each clue.

- Each factor must have 2 or more digits.

- Write your end time, and find your race time.

- Check each other's examples, and compare your race times. The player with all correct examples in the least time wins.

Clues	Examples
Product is a multiple of 2.	
Product has 4 digits.	
Product is greater than 10,000.	
Product is between 800 and 950.	
Product is 1200.	

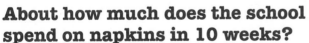

An average of 3000 napkins are used in the school cafeteria each week.

Each package of 300 napkins costs $2.

About how much does the school spend on napkins in 10 weeks?

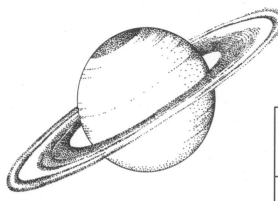

Lengths of Days on Planets

Planet	Day length (to the nearest hour)
Earth	24
Jupiter	10
Mars	25
Mercury	1400
Neptune	16
Pluto	153
Saturn	11

To the nearest hour, the day of one of these planets is about 127 times the length of another planet's day.

What are the 2 planets?

Use all of the digits shown above to write 5-digit numbers.

Make a list of the 5-digit numbers that

* rounded to the nearest thousand equal 42,000.

* rounded to the nearest thousand equal 60,000.

* rounded to the nearest thousand equal 25,000.

Air Miles Between Cities

	London	Paris	Rome	New Delhi	Tokyo
New York	3470	3640	4290	7320	6760
London		210	890	4180	5960
Paris			690	4100	6050
Rome				3690	6140
New Delhi					3640

The Ranas flew from London, England, to New Delhi, India.

The Troys flew from Rome, Italy, to New Delhi, India.

About how many more miles did the Ranas fly than the Troys?

Imagine that you just won $10,000 in 10-dollar bills.

How many 10-dollar bills did you win?

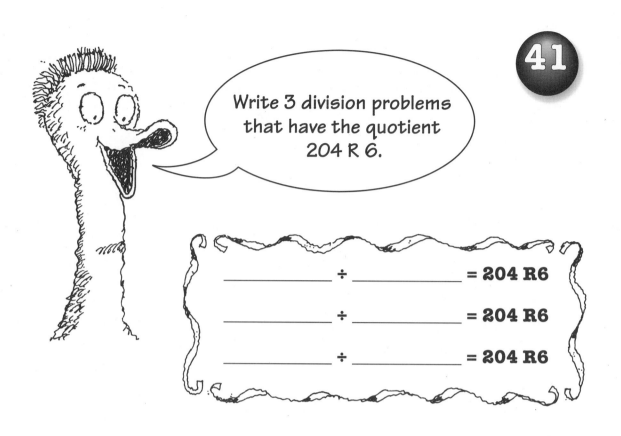

41

Write 3 division problems that have the quotient 204 R 6.

_____ ÷ _____ = **204 R6**

_____ ÷ _____ = **204 R6**

_____ ÷ _____ = **204 R6**

42

An adult elephant weighs about 4.5 tons.

An adult polar bear weighs about 1500 pounds.

About how many times heavier is an adult elephant than an adult polar bear?

You want to buy a lot of bird food.

Which is the better buy?

80 boxes
for $59.98

120 boxes
for $79.98

Tell how you know.

- -

At the beginning of the month, Ms. Chang's bank account showed a balance of $1346.24.

During the month, she deposited $2543.88 and withdrew $3012.18.

What was Ms. Chang's balance at the end of the month?

Margo is planning to take a 917-mile trip by car.

Estimate the number of hours she will need to drive if she averages 45 miles per hour.

Explain how you made your estimate.

- -

Choose numbers from the sign.

Estimate their sums to complete the statements.

Use each number once.

____ + ____ is between 8000 and 9000.

____ + ____ is between 15,000 and 16,000.

____ + ____ is between 5000 and 6000.

____ + ____ is between 12,000 and 13,000.

1046	5216
397	12,921
2198	8321
684	11,498

47

The Improve Our Playground Committee is holding fund-raising events to raise $10,000.

How much more money do they need to raise?

Event	Money Raised
Bake sale	$294.35
Concert	$1003.45
Field day	$682.24
Rummage Sale	$1428.68
Walk-a-thon	$3296.50

48

Use the numbers 0, 1, 2, 3, 4, 5, 6, 7, 8, and 9.

Write one number in each ☐ to get the greatest possible sum.

```
   ☐ ☐ ☐ ☐ ☐
+  ☐ ☐ ☐ ☐ ☐
_____
```

Find each product.

Then complete the next 2 lines.

Describe any patterns you see.

101 × 222 = _____

101 × 2222 = _____

101 × 22,222 = _____

_____ × _____ = _____

_____ × _____ = _____

Mario's dolphin bank is filled with pennies.

He also has 1024 pennies in his piggy bank and 324 pennies in his duck bank.

Mario put all of the pennies in 50-penny rolls and exchanged them at a bank for a $20 bill.

- How many pennies were in Mario's dolphin bank?

- How many rolls of pennies did Mario exchange?

Play this game with a friend.

Take turns, and use different colors.

- Choose one number from A and one from B.
- Estimate A ÷ B.
- Color the quotient on the Game Board.

The winner is the first to get 4 in a row, column, or diagonal.

Game Board

240	24	6	1440
120	18	90	36
60	72	540	8
96	360	20	27

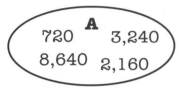

A
720   3,240
8,640   2,160

B
36   120
90   6

The table lists the greatest known depths of the world's 4 largest oceans.

How many feet deeper is the Pacific Ocean than the Arctic Ocean?

Ocean Depths	
Ocean	**Greatest Known Depth (feet)**
Pacific	36,198
Atlantic	27,493
Indian	24,442
Arctic	18,050

The mystery number is on the sign.

The number is

- greater than 10,495 + 6253.

- less than 41,833 − 5072.

- divisible by 9.

The mystery number is _____.

25,857
16,486
40,095
30,624

53

- -

What is the start number?

54

Start
number
?

Divide
by 2

Divide
by 4

Subtract
798

End
number
108

Ticket Sales	
Play	**Tickets Sold**
The Jazz Slinger	2107
Cindermellow	1893
Hanzel and Pretzel	1536
Rumpel Snake Skin	1632
Snow Write	1945

The Children's Playhouse performed 5 plays this year.

Each ticket cost $7.

How much money was collected from ticket sales?

- -

Estimate to answer this question:

Which quotient is greater?

$4927 \div 5$

$4338 \div 4$

Tell how you estimated.

The sum of 2 numbers is 5794.
One number is 2 more than the other number.
What are the 2 numbers?

- -

There are 1275 pennies in the elephant bank.

There are 205 nickels in the cat bank.

How many pennies or nickels would you move from one bank to the other to give the banks the same amount of money?

List the steps you used to answer the question.

Compare your steps with a classmate's.

Estimate.

Draw a ring around 2 numbers in each box.

Their product must be in the range.

251   8900
    150   360
52   2400

Range: 5000–10,000

195   500
200   32
    650

Range: 25,000–50,000

100   320
    460
52   250

Range: 50,000–100,000

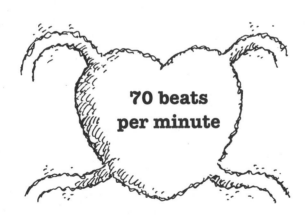

70 beats per minute

Your heart beats about 70 times per minute.

At that rate, about how many times will your heart beat in 10 days?

Use a calculator to help you.

Write a story problem that can be solved by multiplying 2300 and 4 and adding 372 to the product.

Give your problem to a classmate to solve.

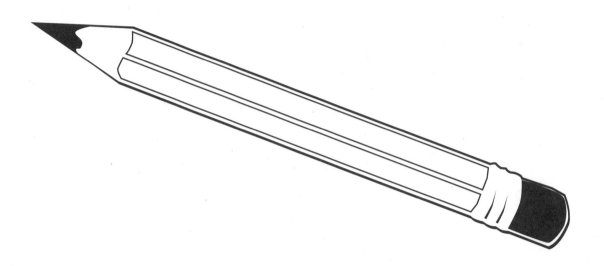

Try this without using pencil and paper or a calculator.

If a box with four stars = 28,000 *and* a box with a triangle and a star = 10,000

then a box with a triangle and three stars = _____ *and* a box with two triangles and six stars = _____

The quotient is 450.

The divisor is 19.

The remainder is 10.

What is the dividend?

- -

Make the sentences true.

Put + or − in each .

Put × or ÷ in each ⬟.

$$801 \; \bigcirc \; 437 \; \bigcirc \; 627 \; \bigcirc \; 199 = 810$$

$$11{,}233 \; \diamondsuit \; 239 \; \diamondsuit \; 516 \; \diamondsuit \; 12 = 2021$$

The place on Earth with the highest elevation is Mt. Everest in Asia. It is about 29,028 feet *above* sea level.

The greatest known depth is the Mariana Trench in the Pacific Ocean. The trench is about 36,200 feet *below* sea level.

How many miles are between the lowest and highest points on Earth?

- -

I am thinking of a 4-digit number.

- The number is between 2000 and 3000.

- When you divide the number by 10, the remainder is 2.

- The hundreds digit and the tens digit are the same.

- The sum of the digits is 12.

The number is _____.

The Sears Tower in Chicago is 1450 feet tall and has 110 stories.

To the nearest foot, estimate the distance between floors in the tower.

Mr. Guen averages 8 hours of sleep each day.

He is 40 years old today.

Estimate the number of years and months of his life he has spent sleeping.

Compare your way of estimating with a classmate's way.

The perimeter of this square-shaped gym floor is 1200 feet.

What is its area?

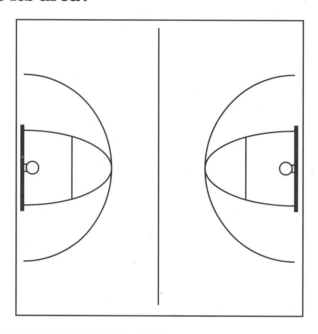

When I started my drive to the lake, my odometer showed (3 2 9 7 8 . 4) **.**

When I reached the lake, my odometer showed (3 3 0 7 9 . 7) **.**

The trip took 2 hours 15 minutes.

Estimate the number of miles I drove per hour.

Estimate.

Raven added 3 of the numbers on the sign.

She got a sum of 1,303,268.

What number did she *not* add?

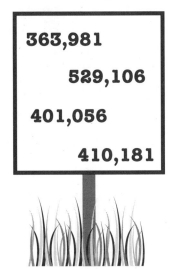

363,981

      529,106

401,056

      410,181

---

8 5 7

  3 2 4

Use each digit shown to make a number.

- The number is between 250,000 and 300,000.
- The digit in the ten-thousands place is divisible by 4.
- The digit in the thousands place is 3 more than the digit in the hundreds place.
- The number is divisible by 5.

The number is _____.

Write your own clues for the number 470,293.

Give your clues to a classmate to find the number.

Brad has to read a 1250-page report for a meeting in 2 weeks.

He began reading 4 days ago and averaged 60 pages per day.

At this rate, will he finish on time? Explain.

- -

Boston to
San Francisco
3090 miles

You leave Boston at 8 A.M. on April 1.

You drive toward San Francisco at an average speed of 50 miles per hour.

You travel for 8 hours a day, including 2 half-hour rest stops.

On what day will you arrive in San Francisco?

$$1 \quad 3 \quad 5 \quad 7 \quad 9$$

Use the digits above to fill the squares.

Use each digit once.

Record the digits to get a quotient between 1400 and 1500.

☐) ☐ ☐ ☐ ☐

Now record the digits to get a quotient between 300 and 400.

☐) ☐ ☐ ☐ ☐

- -

Choose a book in your classroom.

Pick 3 pages in the book.

Count the number of words on each page.

Find the average.

Use this information to estimate the number of words in the book.

When you count by 7s, beginning with 7, will you say 37,777?

Tell how you decided.

Put in decimal points to make the sentence true.

$$14273 + 51962 - 1031 = 1936.61$$

The number pattern continues.

2100	2200								

1100	1200	1300	1400	1500	1600	1700	1800	1900	2000

100	200	300	400	500	600	700	800	900	1000

Follow the arrows to fill in the missing numbers.

400 ↑ = 1400   700 ↑↑↑↓ = 2700

600 ← = 500   900 ↗ = 2000

1700 → → → = _____   1400 ↑↖ = _____

500 ↗ → ↑ ← = _____   3200 ↓↘ ← ↑↘ = _____

- -

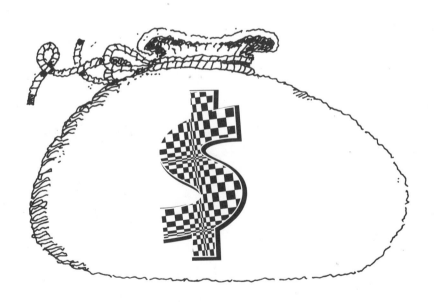

Mr. Spendor inherited $1,000,000.

He spent an average of $500 each day until he had used up his inheritance.

How many years and months did it take Mr. Spendor to spend his inheritance?

The pattern continues.

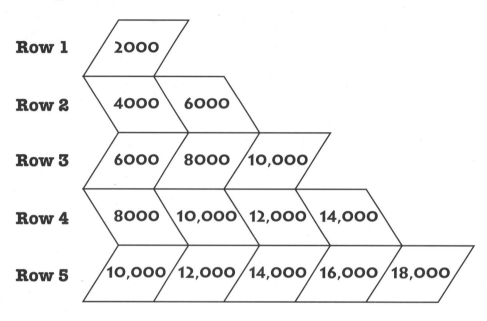

Row 1 — 2000

Row 2 — 4000 6000

Row 3 — 6000 8000 10,000

Row 4 — 8000 10,000 12,000 14,000

Row 5 — 10,000 12,000 14,000 16,000 18,000

What will be the last number in row 12?

Explain your thinking.

- -

Work with a partner.

Take turns.

Use a timer.

When your partner says "go," write as many number pairs as you can with a sum of 10,000.

Your partner must say "stop" after 1 minute.

Compare your strategies for finding number pairs.

Number Pairs with a Sum of 100

Elevator 2315
Safety Regulations
Maximum Capacity
2500 pounds

There are 12 people on the elevator.

Their total weight is 1624 pounds.

At their average weight, how many more people can get on the elevator?

- -

84

Sal's Tech	**TV Mart**
Regular price $468.99	Regular price $583
Now 10% off!	Now 20% off!

The televisions are the same.

Which store offers the better buy?

The volume of this rectangular prism is 1536 cubic inches.

What is its length?

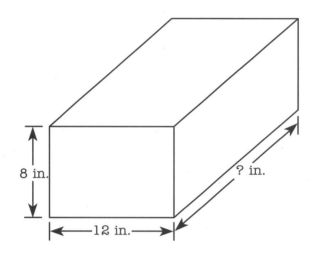

8 in.

12 in.

? in.

- -

8   2730   78   10,920

Choose numbers from the sign to make each equation true.

_____ × _____ = 212,940

_____ ÷ _____ = 1365

_____ × _____ = 624

_____ ÷ _____ = 4

Talk with a classmate about how you made your choices.

Use your calculator.

What is the value of the ?

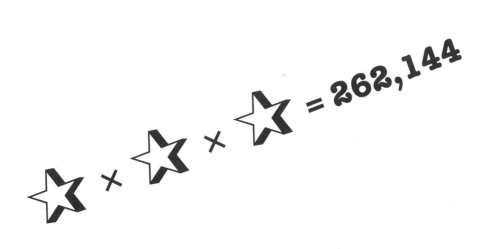 = 262,144

- -

A 100-dollar bill weighs 0.035 ounce.
The bag is filled with 100-dollar bills.
Can you lift the bag?
Explain.

$10,000,000

Of the 9 planets in our solar system, Pluto is the smallest and Jupiter is the largest.

- The diameter of Pluto is 2275 kilometers.

- The diameter of Jupiter is 139,822 kilometers.

How many times the diameter of Pluto is the diameter of Jupiter?

Jupiter

○ **Pluto**

The *motion* in motion pictures is due to the rapid showing of still pictures, called *frames*.

Frames are shown at the rate of 24 frames per second.

What is the total number of frames shown for a 2-hour movie?

Write one subtraction sign in each number sentence to make it true.

1 5 2 7 9 6 4 2 = 14,637

3 2 4 8 1 7 9 4 = 1454

Write one multiplication sign and one addition sign in each number sentence to make it true.

3 4 2 9 4 5 = 13,721

1 7 9 5 3 2 = 927

- -

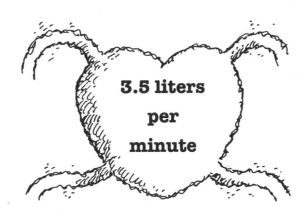

3.5 liters
per
minute

Use a calculator.

Your heart pumps about 3.5 liters of blood in 1 minute.

About how many kiloliters of blood does your heart pump in 1 year?

1000 liters
=
1 kiloliter

The diameter of a quarter is 25 millimeters.

Imagine a line of quarters 1 kilometer long.

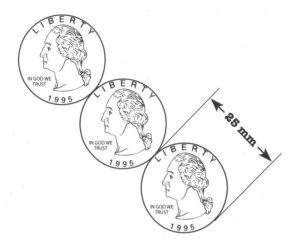

What is the total value of the quarters?

- -

A clock chimes

- once at 1:00
- twice at 2:00
- 3 times at 3:00

and so on until it chimes 12 times at 12:00.

How many times does the clock chime in a leap year?

Show how you found your answer.

What are the 3 numbers?

The product of the 3 numbers is 4200.

The sum of the 3 numbers is 49.

Tell the steps you used to find the numbers.

- -

I'm thinking of a number.

All of its digits are different.

- The thousands digit is equal to the cube of the ten-thousands digit.

- The hundreds digit is half of the ones digit and a third of the tens digit.

- The sum of the digits is equal to 7 times the square of 2.

What is the number?

Which is greater:
2^{10} or 10^2?
Tell how you know!

We're thinking of a number between 500 and 1000.

- When you divide it by 2, the remainder is 0.

- When you divide it by 5, the remainder is 0.

- When you divide it by 7, the remainder is 0.

- When you divide it by 11, the remainder is 0.

What is our number?

The Cycle Shop sells 5 types of cruising bicycles.

The average price of a bike is $297.

Four of the prices are $285, $290, $298, and $300.

What is the price of the fifth type?

Tell how you decided.

- -

One billion seconds is about 32 years.

One trillion seconds is about how many years?

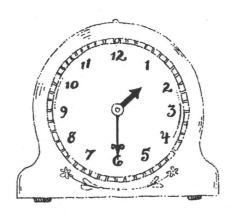

Answers

1. 915, 930, 945, 960, 975, 990

2. The problem is 9439 + 3726 + 2584 = 15,749.

3. yes; Possible explanation:
   $150 + $40 + $10 + $40 + $20 + $20 = $280

4. Answers will vary.

5. Possible answer: His estimate is too low. He needs more than $900.

6. 600.695

7. Possible answer:

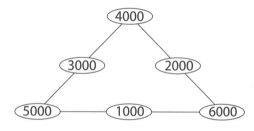

9. Possible questions: How many more pennies than dimes does Maddy have? (1689) What is the value of Max's coins? ($46.15) What is the value of Max's nickels? ($42.70) How much more money does Maddy have than Max? ($6.49)

10. 3549

11. $217.20

12. about $18\frac{1}{3}$ gallons

13.

2724.9	3.5	46.35	(2774.75)
18.7	8687	0.35	(8706.05)
0.1	49.5	1094	(1143.6)
(2743.7)	(8740)	(1140.7)	

14. 34,100

15. 29,000 people

16. 57; Explanations will vary.

18. 618 and 619

19. Answers will vary.

20. Estimates will vary.

21. 100 whole numbers; Explanations will vary.

22. 1188 km

23. The problem is 629 × 24 = 15,096. Explanations will vary.

24. Possible answer: It will take about 2.5 h to drive 110 mi and you want to arrive at 7:15 A.M.; leave at 4:45 A.M.

25. The digit is always 9.

26. Methods will vary; the sum is 42,050.

27. 7000; 112,000

28. row 51; Possible explanation: The last number in each row is 90 times the row number, and 90 × 51 = 4590, so 4580 is the next-to-last number in row 51.

29. Answers will vary.

30. Possible answer: About 2652 mi; it's about 4 times the distance between Dallas and Denver.

31. Clues and resulting numbers will vary.

32. Software Town's offer

33. 46

34. April 12

35. Examples and race times will vary.

36. $200

37. Mercury and Saturn

38. nearest thousand 42,000: 42,068, 42,086; nearest thousand 60,000: 60,248, 60,284, 60,428, 60,482; nearest thousand 25,000: 24,608, 24,680, 24,806, 24,860

39. 490 more miles

40. 1000 bills

41. Problems will vary.

42. about 6 times

43. 120 boxes for $79.98; Possible explanation: For 80 boxes for $59.98, each box costs about 75¢. For 120 boxes for $79.98, each box costs about 67¢.

44. $877.94

45. Possible answer: Since $20 \times 45 = 900$, she will need to drive between 20 and 21 h.

46. $8321 + 397$; $12,921 + 2198$; $5216 + 684$; $11,498 + 1046$

47. $3294.78

48. Possible answer: $97,531 + 86,420$ (The digits at each place-value position can be exchanged.)

49. $101 \times 222 = 22,422$;
$101 \times 2222 = 224,422$;
$101 \times 22,222 = 2,244,422$;
$101 \times 222,222 = 22,444,422$;
$101 \times 2,222,222 = 224,444,422$;
Possible patterns: The answer has two 2s on either end and 4s in the center. The number of 4s is equal to the number of 2s in the second factor, minus 2.

50. 652 pennies, 40 rolls

52. 18,148 ft

53. 25,857

54. 7248

55. $63,791

56. $4338 \div 4$; Possible explanation: $4338 \div 4$ is more than 1000, and $4927 \div 5$ is less than 1000.

57. 2896, 2898

58. Move 125 pennies from the elephant bank to the cat bank. Steps will vary.

59. 52 and 150, 195 and 200, 250 and 320

60. 1,008,000, or about 1 million, times

61. Story problems will vary.

62. 24,000; 48,000

63. 8560

64. $801 + 437 - 627 + 199 = 810$
$11,233 \div 239 \times 516 \div 12 = 2021$

65. about 12.4 mi

66. 2442

67. 13 ft

68. 13 yr 4 mo; Methods will vary.

69. 90,000 ft^2

70. 45 mph

71. 401,056

72. 287,435; Clues will vary.

73. no; Possible explanation: At this rate, 18 days (4 days plus 2 weeks) of reading is only 1080 pages.

74. April 9

75. Answers will vary.

76. Answers will vary.

77. no; Possible explanation: 37,777 is not evenly divisible by 7.

78. $1427.3 + 519.62 - 10.31 = 1936.61$

79. from left to right: 2000, 3300, 2600, 1300

80. about 5 yr 6 mo

81. 46,000; Possible explanation: The first number in each row is double the row number times 1000 (so in row 12 it would be 24,000). Then 2000 is added to that number 11 times (22,000); 24,000 + 22,000 = 46,000.

82. Number pairs and strategies will vary.

83. 6 more people

84. Sal's Tech

85. 16 in.

86. $2730 \times 78 = 212{,}940$ (or 78×2730)

    $10{,}920 \div 8 = 1365$

    $78 \times 8 = 624$ (or 8×78)

    $10{,}920 \div 2730 = 4$

87. 64

88. Answers will vary; the bag weighs 218.75 lb.

89. about 61.5 times

90. 172,800 frames

91. $15279 - 642 = 14{,}637$

    $3248 - 1794 = 1454$

    $3429 \times 4 + 5 = 13{,}721$

    $179 \times 5 + 32 = 927$

92. about 1840 kL

93. $10,000

94. $1 + 2 + 3 + 4 + 5 + 6 + 7 + 8 + 9 + 10 + 11 + 12 = 78$ times/half-day;

    $78 \times 2 = 156$ times/day;

    156 times/day $\times$ 366 days = 57,096 times

95. 14, 15, 20; Explanations will vary.

96. 28,396

97. 2^{10}; Possible explanation: $2^{10} = 1024$ and $10^2 = 100$

98. 770

99. $312; Explanations will vary.

100. 32,000 yr